D0286537

# You Don't Have to Exercise When...

## Sara Parriott

Copyright © 1980 by Sara Parriott
All rights reserved.
Library of Congress Catalog Card No.: 79-91840
Distributor's ISBN: 0-312-91012-6
Publisher's ISBN: 0-87477-177-X
Design by John Brogna
Manufactured in the United States of America
Published by J.P. Tarcher, Inc.
9110 Sunset Blvd., Los Angeles, Calif. 90069
Published simultaneously in Canada by Thomas Nelson & Sons Limited,
81 Curlew Drive, Don Mills, Ontario M3A 2R1
Q  10  9  8  7  6  5  4  3  2  1
First Edition

## INTRODUCTION

Some people actually enjoy strenuous exercise. They claim that lifting weights until their bodies scream with pain makes them "feel good", and they suggest that running until you are ready to throw up is "a high". I call it painful and sickening. Like everyone else, I was lured into exercising with that "Everybody's doing it!" propaganda. After all, who wouldn't want to look like Farrah Fawcett–~~Majors~~; rosy, glistening, and breathless? But I found out that on me, "rosy" meant bright red and blotchy, "glistening" meant buckets of sweat, and "breathless" meant exactly that, without breath.

At this moment you might suspect that I am less than an avid athlete, and you too may be a member of the **L**ots-of-**A**thletes-more-**Z**ealous-than-**Y**ourself Club. Well, that's okay. All of us simply have not reached the point where we enjoy daily exercise. It is neither something we require to start a day nor is it something we eagerly look forward to for relaxation in the evening. We just don't need the stuff – and if it weren't for the massive social pressure to "do something good for your body", we would gladly give the whole thing up. But alas, we can't.

That is why I found it necessary to write this book. There are plenty of books and periodicals for the sweating fanatics who have nothing better to do than run around tracks all day and all night like little hamsters. Those books are very one-sided – all about when and how we should exercise. Something was needed for those of us with a more realistic approach to life. We needed a book that would tell us when NOT TO EXERCISE. After all, what is day without night? Matter without anti-matter? Yin without Yang? And what is exercise without inactivity? Not much. If we don't know how to relax, how will we know when we have exercised?

That, dear reader, is why I have compiled a list of times when inactivity is appropriate; the instances where exercise is ineffective, bad for you, or even downright rude. So take off those sneakers, sit back, and read this book. For, one of the many times you don't have to exercise is...
WHEN YOU'RE IMPROVING YOUR MIND.

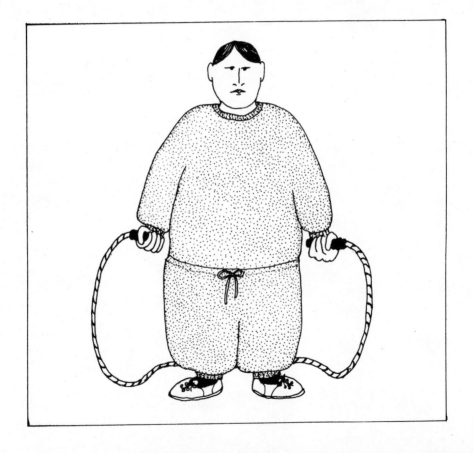

...you took the dog for a walk

. . . it's dark outside

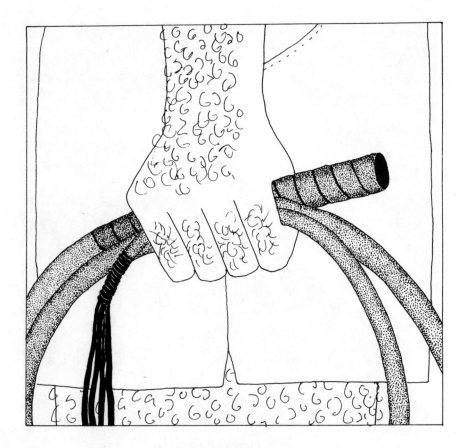

...you don't like the instructor

...you live in a walkup

...it's too hot

...it's too cold

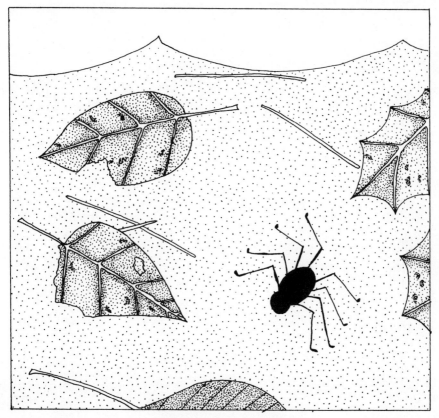

...the water's dirty

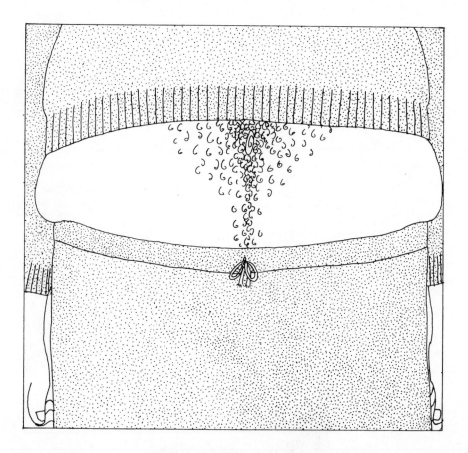

...your exercise show has been preempted

...the class doesn't start until next month

...the gym is closed

... you're out of deodorant

...you're basically an intellectual

...you're on vacation

**A MESSAGE FOR . . . .**

*you're waiting for an important phone call.*

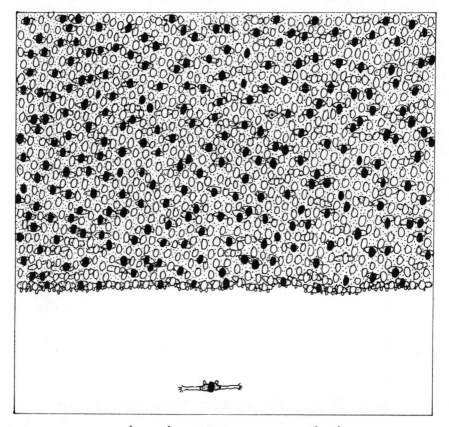

...the class is too crowded

...your friend hurt himself doing it

... you had a long hard day

...you did it yesterday

# You have no other bad habits

...you don't have the right equipment

...you have relatives in from out of town

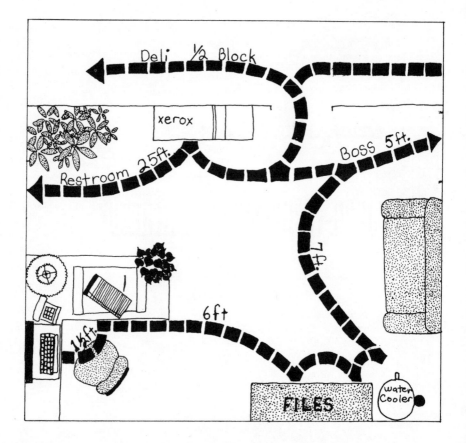

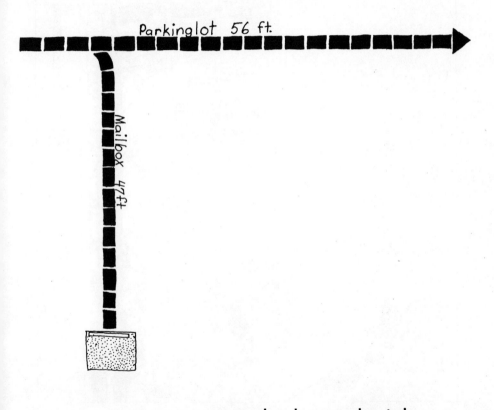

... you move around a lot on the job

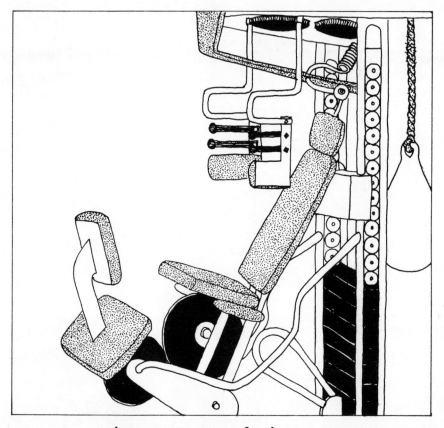

...the equipment frightens you

...you have to lose weight first

## THE TRUE INVASION OF THE BODY SNATCHERS
## — A CALL TO ARMS

In spite of what you have learned so far, you will probably find that there are times when you still feel driven to exercise – such is the perversity of human nature. Unfortunately, these feelings are almost impossible to avoid and not nearly as harmless as they may appear. In fact, under closer examination, they reveal themselves to stem from two complex and debilitating emotions: guilt and vanity.

Society today is patterned so that it does not allow us to shake these disturbing stirrings toward exercise – but, instead, magnifies them, creating an unhealthy atmosphere of anxiety and pressure under which most of us will eventually buckle. A body-obsessed generation controlling the entertainment industry and popular magazines presses the rest of the populace through guilt/vanity propaganda to unnatural amounts of exercise and mindless physical exertion in a wide variety of athletic undertakings. Think about it. How many times have you watched an interview of a famous person, only to be told the number of miles he runs each day – which, of course, has nothing to do with anything but his ego. And why does every actress on television – even battered wives on soap operas – have a body you would die for? And, how many of you really believe that today's fashions were designed for human beings? Only if you call those painted, anorectic mannequins human beings!

Being constantly barraged with this type of demoralizing verbal propaganda and visual imagery, it has become necessary to protect and strengthen our natural, God-given instinct to remain inactive. Just as they diet compulsively to slim themselves and exercise fanatically to build their grotesque, muscle-bound bodies, we must conscientiously exert ourselves to maintain our right to be flabby, thus protecting ourselves against becoming slaves to the rack of a Nautilus machine and prisoners in our own gyms.

In this regard, I can only hope that these few anti-guilt/ vanity suggestions will strengthen your resistance and reinforce the pride you have in your own independent character:

1. Avoid magazine articles on the new fitness craze sweeping the country ("POLITICIANS ON THE RUN", "SWIM-MING ACROSS THE COUNTRY"), but save all articles in which athletes make amazingly stupid comments, exhibit bad sports-manship, and act juvenile and conceited. Especially effective are nostalgic articles on once-famous athletes now living in penurious obscurity.

2. Get rid of any older friends who are in better shape

than you are. Even if this includes your mother. Surround yourself with people who are at least ten pounds overweight and have to catch their breath after taking a shower.

3. Instead of worrying about all those opportunities you have missed out on because of your physical condition (highly paid careers in modeling, celebrity boyfriends or girlfriends, being a celebrity yourself), think about how shallow and unfulfilling careers that rely on looks obviously have to be and how insensitive and materialistic the people are who judge others first by their looks.

4. Keep a list of all injuries and ailments stemming from overexercise and participation in athletic contests.

5. When at a party, watch the overly enthusiastic jogger bore the tears out of everybody with his tales of how it changed his whole life.

6. Think about all the time and money you saved by not having a model's body. For instance, it frees you from keeping up with the latest ridiculous fashions, narrows the confusing fabric options you have to choose from (no horizontal stripes, loud colors, or Spandex), and saves you from spending money and wasting evenings in bars showing yourself off to the opposite sex. What a relief!

7. Understand that not exercising **need not** reinforce your

worst fears about your lack of self-discipline or your deep-seated masochistic tendencies. On the contrary, not exercising shows the strong will of someone who is not afraid to step apart from the crowd, a highly intelligent person who has freed his or her mind of cultural chains and is "above it all."

8. Finally, if you **do** relent and exercise, even if it's only for one day, DON'T TELL ANYBODY! People may think that exercise is important to you and begin to make pleasant inquiries about your progress ("Go swimming today?" "How's the exercise class?"). When you return to a state of natural non-exercise, these comments will be a constant source of guilt and embarrassment.

...you have to give up smoking first

. . . your spouse won't do it with you

# YOU'RE
# INTO
# MEDITATION

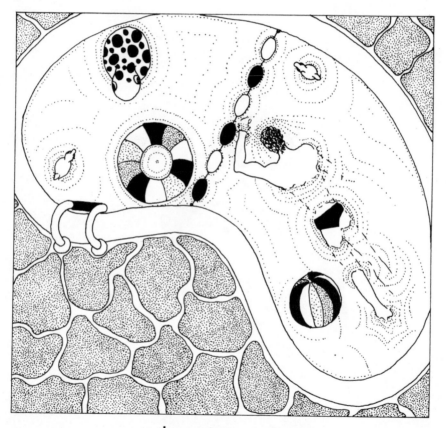

...there is no room

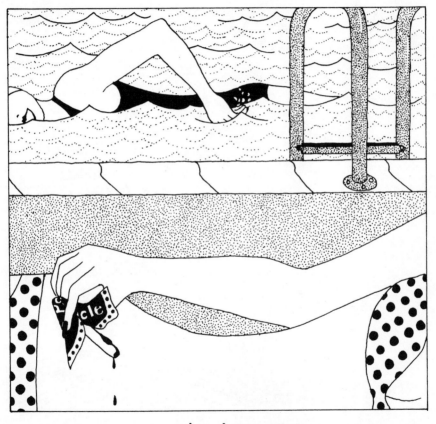

. . . you've just eaten

...you don't have the time

...you've just moved the furniture

. . . you have two or more children under
the age of four

from the desk of
Dr. J. R. Robinson

*you've got an excuse from the doctor.*

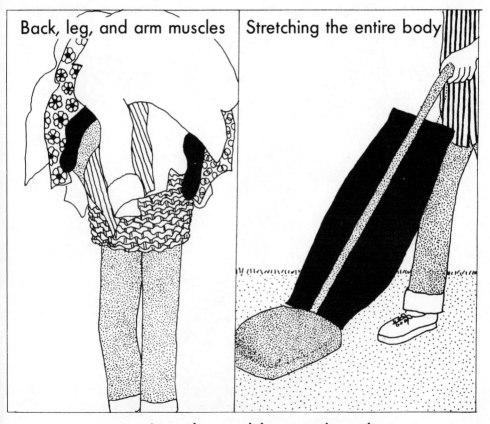

Back, leg, and arm muscles

Stretching the entire body

...you've cleaned house that day

# IT'S DURING THE OLYMPICS

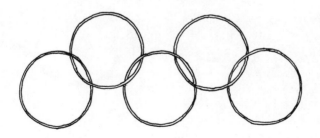

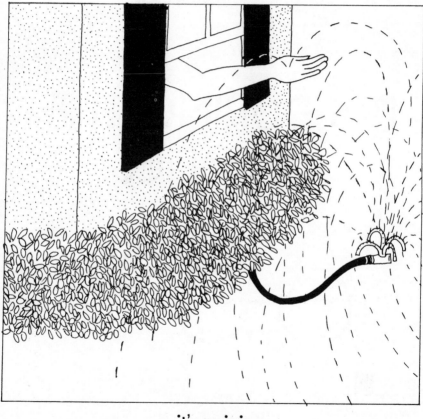

...it's raining

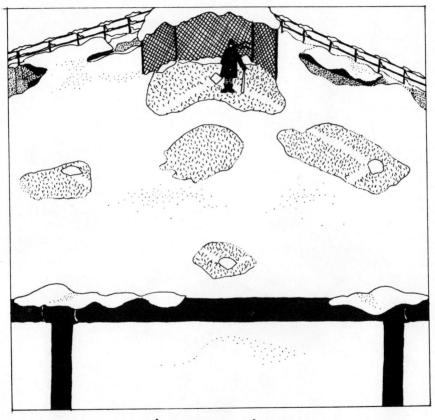

...the season is over

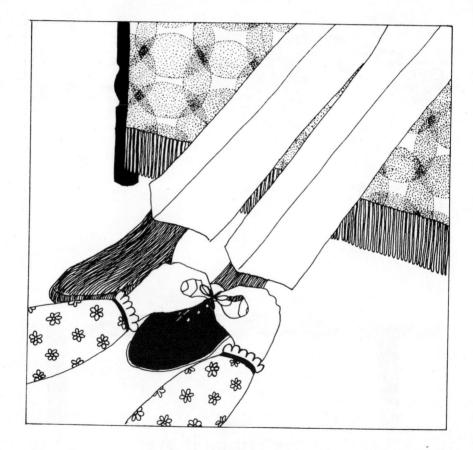

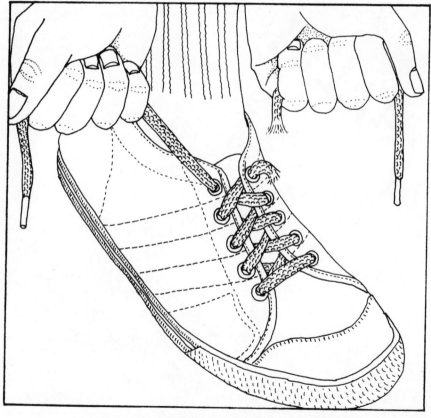

...your equipment isn't working

...it's the Sabbath

...you've heard that it
actually makes your thighs larger

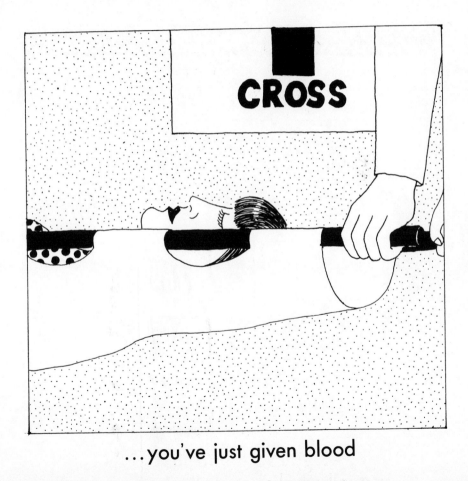

...you've just given blood

...you'll make someone else feel guilty

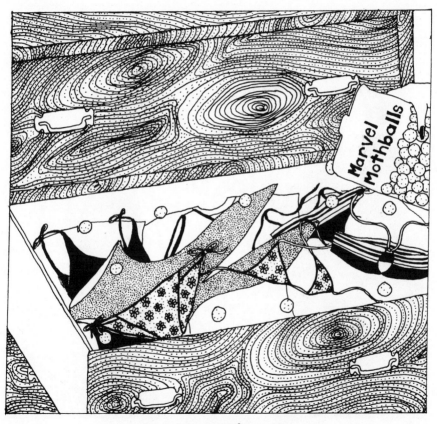

...it's past Labor Day

You're in a
Foreign
Country

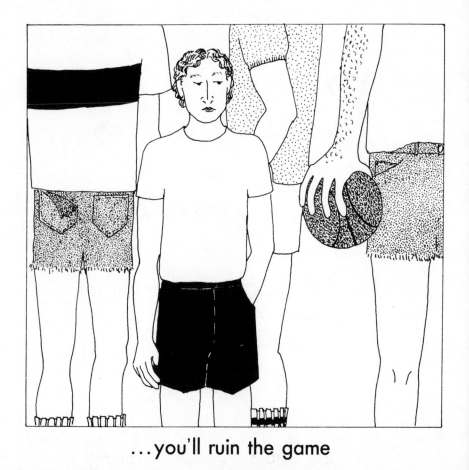

...you'll ruin the game

... your equipment isn't working

...you're hung over

...the ground is wet

Umberto's
The total beauty experience

you've just had

set                    15 00

your hair

done

Total

...you can't afford it